HAVE YOU SEEN
BUGS?

Joanne Oppenheim

ILLUSTRATED BY
Ron Broda

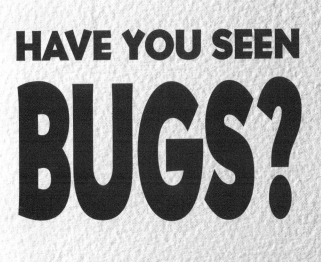

SCHOLASTIC PRESS/New York

To Toni.
—J. O.

To my own little bugs,
Taylor and Eden Broda.
—R. B.

The illustrator would like to thank Joanne Webb for her help with page 30—what a great idea!
Thanks also to William Kuryluk for a wonderful job on the photography.

The illustrations for this book were made with paper sculpture and watercolor. Each layer of paper
was cut, formed, and painted before being glued into place. The finished sculptures were then
carefully lit and photographed to create the final image.

LIBRARY OF CONGRESS CATALOGING-IN-PUBLICATION DATA
Oppenheim, Joanne.
Have you seen bugs? / written by Joanne Oppenheim ; illustrated by Ron Broda.
p. cm.
Summary: Describes in verse a variety of bugs and how they look, behave, and
improve our lives.
ISBN 0-590-05963-7
1. Insects—Juvenile literature. 2. Arthropoda—Juvenile literature. [1. Insects.
2. Spiders. 3. Arthropods.] I. Broda, Ron, ill. II. Title.
QL467.2.066 1997 595.7—dc21 96-46140 CIP/AC

10 9 8 7 6 5 4 3 2 1   8 9/9 0/0 01 02
Printed in Mexico   49
First U.S. edition, May 1998
The text type for this book was set in 20 point Bernhard Gothic Heavy.

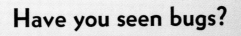

Have you seen bugs?

Itty-bitty bugs
small as specks of sand,

wide-winged bugs
bigger than your hand.

Bugs with stripes
or speckles
or spots,
shiny like metal
or covered with dots.

Iridescent bugs
that shimmer in the light,

winking, blinking bugs
that twinkle in the night.

Dark as bark
green as grass
see-through bugs
with wings like glass.

Shaped like thorns
or sticks
or leaves,

burrowed in bubbles
or clinging to trees.

Hide-and-seek bugs—
can you see these?

6

Watch out for these show-off bugs
with colors bold and bright.
Flashy, sassy, daring bugs
such easy bugs to sight!

Like warning signs,
bold markings say:
I'm poison! I smell!
I sting! Stay away!

Have you seen bugs
and how they move?

Long-legged bugs
jumping with a bound,
short-legged bugs
running on the ground.

Some are fast:
they dart and leap;
some are slow:
they crawl and creep.

Bugs that flutter
and scurry
and dive,
bugs that buzz around a hive.

Walking on the ceiling,
crawling up a wall—
some bugs hardly
move at all!

What about water bugs?
Walking-on-the-water bugs
swimming-under-water bugs
skimming-over-water bugs.

Oaring, soaring,
whirling, twirling,
striding, gliding.
Have you seen these?

Have you heard bugs?

Bugs have no voices
but still they can sing,
rubbing their legs,
whirring their wings.

Busy crickets in thickets
wait for night to fall,
then they rub their legs together
and chirp their mating call.

A bug has no ears
on its little bug head,
but some bugs "hear"
through their legs instead!
While others use antennae

to taste and hear and smell,
and tiny hairs that touch and tell
and help them find their mates as well.
Some bugs even use their feet
to take a taste before they eat!

Have you seen bugs
and how they eat?

Beetles have mouths—
they can bite and chew and snip,
while others like the butterfly
have mouths with straws that sip.

Most bugs dine on plants,
some bugs dine on meat,
others take a nip of blood
or sip on nectar sweet.

Have you seen baby bugs?

Inside a hive,
nesting in hair,
bugs hatch from eggs everywhere.

Underwater, underground,
in so many places
bug eggs are found.

In the bark of trees
or wrapped up in leaves,
baby bugs hatch
from all of these!

Baby bugs are small,
but just for a bit.
Little bugs keep growing
till their skins don't fit.

24

But some bugs form a chrysalis
or spin a fine cocoon,
where abracadabra! they grow wide wings
in a magical changing room.

Have you seen working bugs?

From flower to flower,
bugs work as they go,
carrying pollen
that makes gardens grow.
If it weren't for bugs,
orchards would be bare!
You couldn't have an apple,
an orange or a pear.
There wouldn't be corn
or pumpkins or wheat;
without bugs we'd have little to eat.

Burrowing, weaving
or building a nest,
gathering, guarding,
seldom at rest,

working by day,
working by night,
spinning wondrous webs
or taking off in flight.

Sleek as a needle,
furry as a bear,
so many kinds of bugs
living everywhere!

An army of ants
a flurry of fleas
a band of moths
a swarm of bees
billions of bugs...

Have you seen these?

ABOUT BUGS

Some bugs are insects,
others are not.
Compare their bodies
to find what you've got:
An insect has three parts—
a head at one end
an abdomen in the rear
a thorax in the middle
where wings and legs appear.
An insect has six legs,
no fewer and no more;
some have two wings
but many have four.
Some primitive insects have
no wings at all,
like lice or fleas—they hop or crawl.

The bugs in this book are all arthropods.
They include insects (class Insecta),
spiders (class Arachnida), and millipedes
(class Diplopoda).

CAN YOU SEE THESE BUGS?

The bugs in the text areas are listed from top to
bottom; the ones in the pictures are listed from
left to right.

Page 1 Colorado potato beetle, searcher, yellow
woolly bear, white-marked tussock moth, red ant
worker, fall cankerworm, anise swallowtail, short-
stalked damselfly, rough fungus beetle, oblong-
winged katydid, aphid, golden garden spider

Pages 2-3 Text area: Costa Rican beetle, cotton-
wood borer; Picture: stag beetle, ladybug,
polyphemus moth, ten-lined June beetle

Pages 4-5 Text area: lichen moth, *Brochymena*;
Picture: musk beetle, fire bug, apple-sucker, ant
lion fly, green lacewing, firefly, green stink bug,
darkling beetle

Pages 6-7 Text area: acraea moth, big poplar
sphinx; Picture: titan stick insect, California
cankerworm moth, treehopper, spittlebug, locust
treehopper, eastern tiger swallowtail, northern
walking stick, true katydid, leaf insect, Nebraska
conehead

Pages 8-9 zebra longwing, blister beetle

Pages 10-11 Text area: tropical lubber
grasshopper, weevil; Picture: tropical millipede,
earwig, praying mantis, question mark, silverfish

Pages 12-13 green darner, red skimmer, black
horsefly

Pages 14-15 European water spider,
backswimmer, water strider, house mosquito larvae
and pupae, small whirligig beetle, western
mountain gomphid dragonfly, water stick insect,
golden mayfly

Pages 16-17 Text area: periodical cicada, click
beetle; Picture: Mormon cricket

Pages 18-19 male African moon moth

Pages 20-21 Text area: *Nessaea aglaura*; Picture:
nine-spotted ladybug beetle, summer mosquito

Pages 22-23 field cricket and eggs, golden
garden spider and egg sac, tomato hornworm moth
with braconid wasp cocoons on its back, lacewing
eggs, may beetle larva, harlequin cabbage bug and
eggs, lady beetle eggs, honey bee eggs, larvae,
drones, workers, queen

Pages 24-25 monarch butterfly—caterpillar,
chrysalis, adult

Pages 26-27 Text area: shamrock spider, bark
beetle tunnels; Picture: crater-nest ant, honey bee

Pages 28-29 Text area: privet hawkmoth
caterpillar, golden northern bumblebee; Picture:
garden spider

Page 30 All the bugs on this page can be found
elsewhere in the book—except for one mystery
bug invented by the illustrator. Can you spot the
fake?

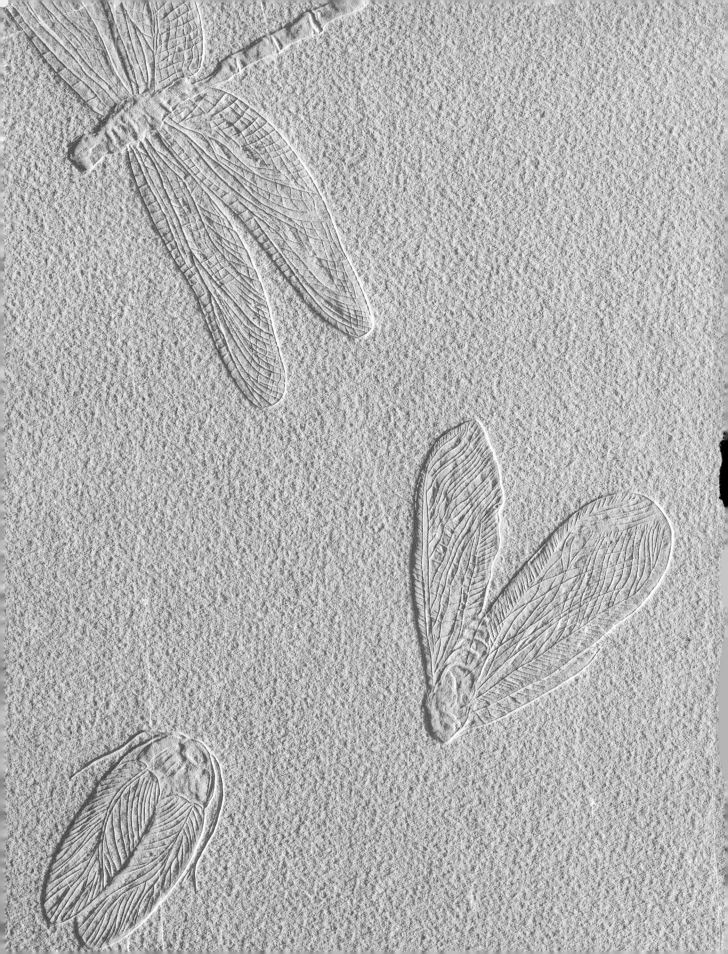